Also by Maureen Roffey

What's the Time?
How Many?
How Do We Get There?
Home Sweet Home
Look, There's My Hat!

This edition first published in Great Britain in 1995 by Macmillan Children's Books, a division of Macmillan Publishers Limited, Cavaye Place, London SW10 and Basingstoke and associated companies worldwide.

ISBN 0 333 58343 4 (hb)

ISBN 0 333 59234 4 (pb)

A CIP catalogue record for this book is available from the British Library.
Printed in Singapore.

What's the Weather?

Maureen Roffey

MACMILLAN CHILDREN'S BOOKS

What is the weather like today?

The wind is blowing.

What is the weather like today?

It is snowing.

What is the weather like today?

It is icy.

The pond is frozen.

What is the weather like today?

It is stormy.

There is thunder and lightning.

What is the weather like today?

It is raining.

What is the weather like today?

The sun is shining.

Come and play!